Smoker

Tainted Love

Diary of a Smoker

Tina Triano

Illustrated by Melanie Cavasin

Ⓢ ENTIENCE PUBLISHING
Oakville, Ontario, Canada

Copyright © Tina Triano 2006

First published in 2006 by Sentience Publishing
3-1500 Upper Middle Road
P.O. Box 76064
Oakville, Ontario L6M 1G0 Canada

www.taintedlovediary.com

Printed in Canada

Library and Archives Canada Cataloguing in Publication

Triano, Tina, 1962-
    Tainted love : diary of a smoker / written by Tina Triano ; illustrated by Melanie Cavasin.

Includes index.
ISBN 0-9781154-0-6

    1. Smoking cessation--Humor. I. Cavasin, Melanie, 1962- II. Title.

HV5740.T75 2006   616.865'060207   C2006-904728-6

CONTENTS

vii	*What Have I Done to Deserve This?*
1	*Every Day I Write the Book*
6	*Simply Irresistible*
8	*The Glamorous Life*
12	*Somebody's Watching Me*
15	*King of Wishful Thinking*
21	*The Final Countdown*
24	*It's So Easy*
28	*Don't Forget Me*
31	*Every Breath You Take*
34	*Message In a Bottle*
37	*Church of the Poison Mind*
41	*All Cried Out*
43	*That's What Friends Are For*
45	*Witchy Woman*
48	*Turn Back the Clock*

50	*Do They Know It's Christmas?*
52	*Back in the High Life Again*
54	*You Don't Own Me*
57	*It's the End of the World as We Know It*
60	*Mother's Little Helper*
64	*Second Chance*
68	*Hurts So Good*
72	*The Riddle*
76	*Pour Some Sugar on Me*
79	*Eat It*
81	*Danger Zone*
83	*Video Killed the Radio Star*
85	*Always Something There to Remind Me*
88	*Whiter Shade of Pale*
92	*Fight For Your Right to Party*
95	*Weird Science*
98	*Melt With You*
101	*Patience*
104	*Papa Don't Preach*
109	*Drive*
112	*Six Months in a Leaky Boat*
117	*Just Another Day*
120	Dedication

WHAT HAVE I DONE TO DESERVE THIS?
PET SHOP BOYS

This song title is my way of saying, "If I thank you at the front of the book, will you forgive me for what I said about you inside?"

Worry not, my friends — I'll be gentle.

There are so many instances, even small nuances, where people had no idea they were a great help to me during all of this — the preparation, the quitting, the writing, the coping.

In some instances it was something that was said many years before this attempt and it just sort of loitered in my head until the time was right for it to replay.

Linda built me a writing room in our last house because it's always been a dream of mine to write a book. I thought that when I did finally write a book it would be a psychological thriller. I may not have been that far off the mark after-all — YOU decide! So, Linda, although I didn't actually do any writing in THAT room before we moved, knowing you had faith in me to write one AT ALL stuck with me and made this book possible.

Melanie, my illustrator and 'sister,' you really put the book to action with your drawings — I am grateful for your talent!

And then there's Suzanne, my colleague and "agent". Her insight and knowledge of the publishing industry from her past life made it possible for me to get this to the market.

There have been numerous cheerleaders on my sideline and coaches in my corner (these sports references are so men find the book palatable). I will not attempt to list everyone, so please feel free to write yer OWN darn book and leave me off YOUR acknowledgment page!

And as I don't want to hurt anyone's feelings, I will list in alphabetical order those to whom I owe an additional debt of gratitude (and no percentage of royalties): A.J. (my Dad), Bob, Brendan, Bruce, the entire Cavasin family, Deb, Jessie, Dr. K., Henry, Lori, Manfred, Norma, PM Designs, Stan, Susan, and Tara (my editor).

And to everyone who visited my website www.taintedlovediary.com and signed my Guestbook with inspiring, heartfelt messages, and pre-ordered books, I consider you all my 'peeps,' and I adore you.

Thank you!

EVERY DAY I WRITE THE BOOK
ELVIS COSTELLO

Tainted Love is my diary.

I am virtually unknown (outside of my personal fan base!). So why would *my* diary be of interest to anyone?

- For 34 years I was a passionate pack-a-day smoker
- For the past nine years I've been a passionate fundraiser for a hospital that just opened a cancer centre
- Since I quit smoking 18 months ago, I've passionately written it all down

I credit my internally conflicting points of view for making this story humorous.

I loved smoking
…but…

TAINTED LOVE

I hated being a smoker.

I wanted to be an ex-smoker
…but…
I didn't want to quit.

I can finally afford to smoke
…but…
I hate spending my money on cigarettes.

You can see my dilemma.

- Do you hold this book hoping it will motivate you to quit smoking?
- Do you turn the pages hoping for some humor?
- Are you a friend of mine and I sent you a signed copy for Christmas and now you're stuck proving you actually read it?

If your reason for reading this is as part of your quit smoking process, I specifically made the chapters short for your sake. I am well aware that your attention span is going to be the same as a two year old's.

From a writer who might be described as focus-deprived, to you — a reader who may be in the same boat — I send my lo…… Has anyone seen my pen?

Now where was I…? Oh, yes — some clarifications….

I was asked why the sub-title of my book was Diary of a Smoker, not Diary of an Ex-Smoker. I answered that just as an alcoholic is not an ex-alcoholic, this will always be my demon. It will only take one cigarette to throw me back there.

You will also have noticed that the chapters are named after retro song titles.

Music has always been central to my life. I'm sure I'm not alone in my non-hallucinogenic-related flashback to periods of life when a song jumps out at me.

I would guess if you're a baby boomer, you could clearly pull from your own memory bank being 12 and feeling geeky and out of place at a gymnasium dance.

Close your eyes and think back…. C'mon, humor me — girls, can you see yourselves saying yes to the last dance? I'll bet the song is *Stairway to Heaven*.

And, ladies — instead of dreamy-eyes across the room, whom you've been fantasizing about all night long (Did he just look at me? Did you see that? I think he looked at me!) you are instead having to spend the longest song in history being groped by a guy who is three inches shorter than you because he's a friend of the family.

Thus proving my theory — for the rest of your days, you will hear *Stairway to Heaven* and *think* Geeky Awkward Moments in a Gymnasium.

You see where I'm going with this?

As I went through my nicotine withdrawal, one thing was constant — my mind continued to cope by reaching out for a song to nosh on.

For me, retro tells the story.

Tainted Love is all about marking time — perhaps the most powerful year-long period of time in my life, so far.

I am creeping toward my mid 40s and although I consider myself on the cusp of the boomer generation, I've been told I'm really a Gen X-er. Regardless, I grew up during a time when smoking was naughty but not the social atom bomb that it is today.

Through every stage of this process, I found distraction where I could, motivation where I least expected, and humor only eventually!

Let me add that it's likely this is the *only* book I will publish in this lifetime. But like any good Leo, I was born feeling that what I have to say is profound and worthy of jotting down.

At various points throughout this book you will see my bubble (head?) thoughts, which I refer to as UM (un-related musing).

> *Sample UM*
> Speaking of bubbles, have you ever considered who invented putting a little plastic wand in dish soap to blow bubbles and charging $3 for 15 cents worth of materials — BRILLIANT!

My reason for doing this is two-fold:
- First, as mentioned, if this is to be my only published work, I want it to have ALL of my profundity included.

- Second, my short attention span these days requires me to 'get it off my chest,' lest my brain fills up with these thoughts and just blows up!

Disclaimer: Feel free to ignore these bubbles if you wish. They exist for ME and may prove distracting.

And for any investors out there, I am presently seeking capital to launch *Tainted Love* nicotine detox centers as a franchise!

Group Counseling Meets '80s Karaoke Night!

Following that, there will be the reality TV series where we can watch people's minds unravel during the detox process in the Twisted Sister house.

And finally, there's the big screen movie starring Sandra Bullock (as Linda, whom you will meet shortly) and Queen Latifah (playing me).

Yo, Queen — call me, we'll do lunch.

Life is good.

SIMPLY IRRESISTIBLE
ROBERT PALMER

I started smoking at age eight. Let me first say, "Sorry, Dad." I realize your belief has been that my first cigarette was the one you caught me smoking in the park when I was 14. Unfortunately, by then, I was a seasoned pro, buying 'fags' and smoking like I was born with one between my 'not-yet-yellow' fingers.

I loved the smell of tobacco, be it cigarettes, cigars, pipe tobacco — oh yes, flashback: Borkum Riff Cherry Tobacco. Mmmmm, the die-hard smokers out there (pun certainly not intended!) know the whiff-of-Riff, of which I speak.

My oldest brother had a box of Tueros cigars in his bedroom. This box consisted of two rows of silver tubes in which evil and temptation had made their home. They were a rare and special treat for him I now assume, because it seemed that by the time he got married and left the house, he still hadn't reached the empty tubes on the lower row — or at least I never heard the ensuing fallout.

There I was, all of 4 feet tall, standing over the toilet in the basement bathroom, not only lighting my first stogie, but inhaling it, and FINISHING it (I was a stealer and a smoker, but NOT wasteful). I wish I could tell you that I immediately gagged, hurled and swore never to go near that filth again. On the contrary, I don't recall feeling lousy when I smoked that first one.

Since that time I have often wondered how my life might have been different had I turned green and used the toilet for more than discarding the only remnant from my first foray into smoking–one small leaf pinched between my fingers.

You would likely now be holding in your hands my cookbook, *400 Ways to Cook Kraft Dinner*, or *Karaoke for Dummies*.

THE GLAMOROUS LIFE
SHEILA E.

But alas, that first smoke was a sweet smoke, as was every darn cigarette for the next 34 years.

For the next three years, my preference changed from *Export A* to *DuMaurier*, just because it was easy pickings from the packs of other family smokers — my Mom and my brother.

Then came the day when I was about 17 and I ran out of smokes at a barn dance. I was with my date Mike in high school and he was a few years older than me. I thought he was the coolest, but when he gave me an extra pack of his *Player's Filter* (one step away from filterless 'rawbacks'), I *did* want to gag this time. Instead, I swallowed the lump in my throat, swigged some beer to quell the burning pit that was now my chest, and chose to act cool instead.

This describes the first few moments of smoking the brand I

would smoke for the next quarter century.

In my high school years, we actually had a 'smoking court.' All the cool people hung out there, bummin' smokes or a 'quick drag' between classes. There was always the girl with lipstick who took a quick drag then handed back that mushy, red, sticky cigarette… icky.

However, like everyone who smoked, I dabbled with other brands.

I recall how we all had to smoke *More* cigarettes for a time because we looked so glamorous with that skinny, long, dark cigarette gently balanced between our fingers. Eventually, and quickly, that kick ended when the fact that it tasted like rolled up poops eventually won out over the glam factor.

My best friend's Mom smoked *Craven M* menthol cigarettes, so I had a very brief stint with those. I found out years later that she switched to menthol because she knew we couldn't stand the taste — and thus wouldn't steal them!

I tried *Vantage* because they had neat little holes in the filter. You also blew up like a puffer fish trying to get any semblance of smoke into your lungs!

When cigarette prices soared in my late twenties, I started smuggling my smokes by the carton across the border, where I purchased them weekly at an Indian reservation in the U.S.
Apparently the mob was doing the same because the smuggling got so out of hand, the prices in Canada dropped again.

TAINTED LOVE

I had a brief stint rolling my own. I don't care if it's the same tobacco, same papers, same filter — it's NOT the same cigarette if you have to WORK for it!

When prices went up again the year before I quit, I smoked no-name brands with equal tar and nicotine but half the price of my beloved *Player's Filter*.

But alas, again, there IS a difference, and I was to be a loyal, faithful consumer who had found her true calling in the blue and white pack with a picture of a sailor on it.

My memories of smoking as a youngster are sporadic, likely because I just saw smoking as an extension of myself.

However, there are two clear visuals I get from the high school years that relate to smoking.

Deb was a careless smoker. When she reads this, she's likely to disagree…. Sorry, Deb, anyone who knew you as a smoker will concur with my assessment.

She must not have liked actually holding cigarettes because shortly after lighting each one, she would put it in an ashtray. And she didn't put it in the ashtray the safe-smoker way with the heater resting on the bottom of the ashtray. No, Deb rested her cigarette at a 90 degree angle in the little ashtray groove.

Well, her luck ran out one night when she stepped outside to chat with an old friend and the cigarette burned down to nothing, rolled out of the groove and fell between the armchair cushions and caught fire. I can still see myself coming up her driveway and saying, "Deb, is that smoke coming out of your living room?" The next 30 minutes were spent trying to get a smoldering three-foot-wide over-stuffed chair through a two-foot door.

> *UM*
> Why on earth would the ashtray inventor put grooves along the periphery of the bowl portion — they actually encouraged bad smoker behavior like that exhibited by Deb... what were you thinking?

The other visual is my sister and I sitting in front of the fireplace, huddled with our shoulders inside the grate, blowing our cigarette smoke up the chimney so Dad wouldn't know we smoked. This was almost as falsely deceptive as borrowing Dad's non-smoking car in the winter, cracking the window an inch, and moving my lips directly toward that crack while blowing the smoke in a pointed fashion, so he wouldn't know I was smoking in his car.

And by the way, Dad, I know what you're thinking, and the answer is YES!

I AM too old to get grounded.

SOMEBODY'S WATCHING ME
ROCKWELL

Just as people have nervous gestures, tics and idiosyncrasies that are unique to them, smokers can be identified in the same way. Do you know one or more of these people?

Guilty – Classic Nouveau
I know who you are, and you know who you are — skulking around taking drags of OPCs (other people's cigarettes) so you can tell your spouse and your kids you don't smoke. You should be ashamed of yourself, letting the smoker take the rap. Perhaps you even join in when non-smokers bash the smokers and react with a pooh-pooh face when one walks by.

Chain Gang – Pretenders
This guy lit a cigarette in 1957 and has lit every one after that with the heater off the one before it. To be sure that you truly are identifying a member of the Chain Gang, check the skin between the

pointer and middle finger just south of the nail bed... can you spell yellow?

Fashion – David Bowie
This gal thinks that if she barely touches the very, very end of the filter with the very, very ends of her fingers, it will act as an accessory to her outfit.

Hold on Tight – Electric Light Orchestra
This cowboy holds on with a thumb and two fingers, so it don't git away on 'im.

Hold on Loosely – .38 Special
This smoker requires a spouse to follow closely behind.

I Can't Wait – Nu Shoes
15 minutes for a break and it takes 10 minutes of travel time to the smoking area.

Nervous Night – Hooters
This cigarette on the morning after will either make you all better, or green.

Against the Wind – Bob Seger
The guy lights every cigarette with a full cupped hand around the end, whether there's a breeze or not.

One Night Love Affair – Bryan Adams
I always wanted to be this kind of smoker — she has a few when she's out with smoking friends but doesn't buy or smoke

them at any other time.

Pass the Dutchie – Musical Youth
Share-zeez – only non-lipstick wearers need apply.

Roll With It – Steve Winwood
They smoke rollies (roll your own) either because it's cheaper, or because they hate when a filter gets between the raw tobacco taste and their not-so-pink-anymore lungs.

Rocket – Def Leppard
This is a rollie made by hand without the benefit of the machine….big fat candy wrapper.

Holding Out for a Hero – Bonnie Tyler
This gal likes to bum a smoke but waits for her brand of choice.

Urgent – Foreigner
Five minutes between meetings and the next meeting is two hours long.

Welcome to the Jungle – Guns n' Roses
This is the smoker's version of the water cooler. Usually no more than three to five people, they discuss the weekend, last night's TV or how much they hate ex-smokers.

KING OF WISHFUL THINKING
GO WEST

I can no longer count the number of times I have tried to quit smoking.

Over the years, I have tried the following:

- Nicotine Gum (BEFORE it was mint flavored)
- Anti-depressant prescription
- Reiki
- Shame
- Hickory Flavored Inhaler
- Nicotine Patch
- Cold Turkey
- Hypnotism
- Meditation
- Cutting Down Number of Cigarettes
- Being Really, Really Sick

- Cutting Down Tar and Nicotine count by Changing Brand
- Self-Help Books
- Self-Help Tapes & CDs
- Websites
- Oral Substitutes (git yer mind outta the gutter, I meant candy!)
- Promise of a Trip to the Bahamas if I Quit for One Year

Some of these earlier attempts to quit require closer examination.

Shame

This was always the hardest one to deal with but quite possibly the most effective. Being disgusted with yourself is not a good place to be, so as you can imagine, I would make every attempt to leave this mindset. The problem is that removing shame could only be accomplished in one of two ways, as I saw it:

1. Choose NOT to have that cigarette that will make you the weak-willed, second-hand smoke-causing shameful creature; or
2. Decide that the REAL shame lay in being controlled by the fascist non-smoking totalitarians that were trying to exert control over my very being.

Guess which road I traveled most often?

Hypnotism

I tried two different versions of hypnotism over the years — a living, breathing hypnotist, and a 'stress-reduction' CD. The latter had some benefit. The former left me smoking more than when I started!

In my very first appointment, during the 15-minute 'interview' portion, he actually got angry with me because I said I wanted to 'try to quit.' In his mind (he falls into the category of the guy I was talking about in point #2 above), I was to either decide to quit or not — I chose NOT!

Cutting Down or Switching to a Lighter Brand

These are just math exercises:

Before Quit Date
> 2 milligrams of nicotine + 12 milligrams of tar = 14 milligrams of stuff that's bad for me X 25 times per day = 350 bad stuffs

Day One of Cutting Down
> 2 milligrams of nicotine + 6 milligrams of tar = 8 milligrams of stuff that's bad for me X 25 times per day = 200 bad stuffs

So obviously by choosing a lighter brand, I have reduced my smoking by almost half!

Math is obviously not my thing....

Really Sick

This one is the hardest to explain to others. A two pack-a-day smoker ends up in intensive care for four months in a coma. He basically sleeps through any physical withdrawal he might otherwise have gone through, wakes up, gets out of bed, and drags his IV pole outside in the snow to have a cigarette.

Non-smokers think to themselves, "You had the perfect opportunity to quit — you were already four months into it… why on earth would you start smoking again?"

Simple answer, "Because I'm a smoker, and it's no different than if I were a fiddle player when I went into the coma and afterwards wanted to pick up the fiddle to feel like 'me' again."

Trip to Bahamas

My Dad made me an offer I couldn't refuse when I was in my twenties. "Quit smoking for one year and I will pay for you to take an all-inclusive trip to the Bahamas."

"Piece of cake," I said.

I went to a travel agent, picked up a brochure of all the best resorts and a bag of red Twizzlers, dropped the smokes I had into the garbage and went on my merry way.

I actually found this attempt (one of my first attempts to quit) not so hard. I suppose having only smoked for about 15 years at that point made a difference.

When I wanted a cigarette, I ate licorice and looked at the resorts in my travel book instead.

Somewhere around three months into it, a great deal came up and a friend asked me to go to the Bahamas with her. I approached my Dad, clear in my conviction that I was now a non-smoker, and said, "I'll still stay a non-smoker for the year but can I take the trip now?" Being a trusting soul, he sent me on my way with my early reward.

Somewhere between booking the trip and arriving at the airport, I apparently made a conscious decision to buy a carton of cigarettes at customs to take with me. My lying, cheating duplicitous head said, "I'll just smoke on my vacation and quit again when I get back... In fact, it was easy 3 months ago, it won't be any harder when I get back!"

Dad would not be the wiser.

The bummer about logic like that is that it assumes addicts actually have some control.

Though I failed at many of these attempts, each one was preparing me mentally for the next attempt.

Sometimes the failures made me resolve NEVER to quit.

It went like this in my mind:

"I can't go through this again. I can't keep beating myself up like this. I was happier as a smoker. Why can't everyone just leave me alone and let me enjoy my life? It IS still MY life, isn't it?"

Something in the back of my mind has been preparing to quit since that first drag, so very long ago.

> *UM*
> Have you ever heard anyone complain about second-hand marijuana smoke? Yeah, I didn't think so...

I am a believer that each attempt led me one step closer to my current ex-smoker status.

Though every attempt has its own book waiting to be written (heaven forbid!), this account focuses on this, my most successful attempt.

And by the way, yes, I did have to pay my Dad back for the trip.

THE FINAL COUNTDOWN
EUROPE

"If you were so darn happy," Reader interjects here, "why did you quit smoking?"

That's the $64,000 question, and I have more than one answer, if I'm being honest...

- Linda, with whom I have lived for more than 10 years, wanted to quit. As anyone who lives with a smoker knows, there will be no peace in a home with one smoker and one EX-smoker.
- Though I could finally afford to smoke, I was beginning to twitch every week when I handed over yet another $75 for a carton of cigarettes. Thinking back to my cab-driving, living-at-the-YWCA days (THAT'S another book altogether!), I was lucky to net $75 in a week of 14-hour days driving in Niagara Falls. And though I was now earning

more than a decent living, it pained me to hand over that money week after week. Let's face it — I'm 43 and at today's cost, my 35 years of smoking would amount to $136,500!

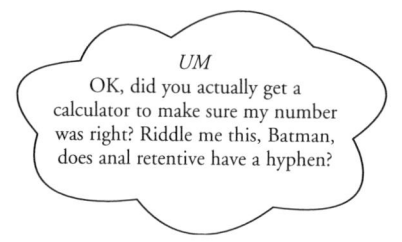

> *UM*
> OK, did you actually get a calculator to make sure my number was right? Riddle me this, Batman, does anal retentive have a hyphen?

- A fine gent by the name of Henry described in vivid detail the last days of a friend of his with lung cancer who lost his life painfully struggling to take every short and labored breath
- Like most people (and ALL Leos!) I hate being controlled, even if it's ME controlling ME. I shiver thinking back to life events planned around the smoke break by...
    - Visiting smoking friends more than non-smoking friends
    - Determining my wardrobe for the day based on knowing I would have many moments of standing outside in inclement weather
    - Not scheduling any meetings between 10:30 and 11:00 in the morning when I would be lighting up for the first time since coming into work in the morning.

It was at this point, in late Fall 2004, that I started to hint around that I was thinking of quitting (Yes, again! What, are ya COUNTING?!) and my motivators stepped up to the plate!

THE FINAL COUNTDOWN

IT'S SO EASY
GUNS N' ROSES

My team of cheerleaders was second to none.

Disclaimer: Any list I could make would be exhaustive but surely I'd forget to mention someone. I would then be eaten alive by guilt, causing me to stress out to the point of smoking again! I KNOW you don't want THAT, so instead I'll sign a copy of this book just to make sure you know you were part of my pain and suffering, and/or recovery!

Bruce was one of the people who motivated me when I was preparing my mind for the quit.

His rank as a self-admitted fellow Attention Deficit Disorder personality and ex-smoker, convinced me that if I followed in his footsteps, I would succeed.

Two of his suggestions…

- a book that would make quitting easy, and
- a hypnosis CD that would help me deal with stress

The book explained that thinking I was 'sacrificing' something by quitting smoking would negate my ability to quit. It went on further to explain that if I saw quitting as the ONLY thing to do, and that it ISN'T such a big deal, it could be — should be — easy. This book also worked for my colleague Rachel. This book would be my savior. This book would be my magic weapon.

So, as I got to the end of the book, about a week before Q minus Zero, (that's QUIT DAY to the civilian), I had THE PLAN.

I also read some anti-smoking websites and Health Canada stuff. In response to their information, I spent a couple days tracking my cigarettes, what I was doing, who I was with, what I felt, etc., so I could determine when I smoked for craving, and when I smoked for stress, social or other reasons.

I found this exercise interesting because I realized prior to quitting that the nicotine withdrawal would likely be the least of my problems — a further hint (or FOREBODING, had I chosen to take heed!) that my addiction MIGHT BE more mental that physical in its nature.

I also reduced my tar and nicotine intake by slowly going from *Player's Filter* to *Player's Light*, to *Player's Extra-Light* to *Player's Silver*. Bruce suggested that this helped make the nicotine withdrawal less harsh on quit date.

This 'cutting down' theory was counter to the suggestions of the book but I had already started cutting back by the time I read that I shouldn't be cutting back.

On a bad day, this might have otherwise caused me to decide this was NOT the right time to quit because I had not prepared properly — as we smokers know, there's always New Year's Eve again!

But I prevailed.

At the conclusion of 'the good book,' I typed out some positive affirmations for myself...

CONGRATULATIONS!
I AM FREE FROM SMOKING!
THIS IS LIKELY THE BIGGEST SUCCESS OF MY LIFE!
MY BANK ACCOUNT WILL BE ENORMOUS!
I AM MY HAPPIEST AS A NON-SMOKER!
I HAVE NEVER FELT AS GOOD AS I DO IN THIS MOMENT!
THIS IS ACTUALLY VERY EASY!
I KNOW I WILL NEVER SMOKE AGAIN!
I AM STRONGER THAN I EVER IMAGINED!
THIS DECISION IS A GREAT ONE!
I AM INCREDIBLY RELIEVED THAT I DON'T SMOKE!
I INSPIRE OTHER PEOPLE WITH MY STRENGTH!
I WISH EVERYONE KNEW HOW GREAT THIS IS!
I AM VERY PROUD OF MYSELF!
I AM A BETTER PERSON!
I AM FINALLY FREE!
I AM A NON-SMOKER!

I laminated a bunch and I placed them everywhere that I might wish for a cigarette: car visor, at office computer, at home computer, bedside, dresser drawers, bathrooms, closets, briefcase, glove compartment, trunk, underwear drawer, kitty litter (Linda, I put that one in here just for you so that you could say, "You'd never *find* it if it was in the kitty litter!")

DON'T FORGET ME WHEN I'M GONE
GLASS TIGER

Q Minus One – the dreaded day (D-day, if you will). The day BEFORE you quit. Your last full day as a smoker. From the Q Minus One perspective, these 24 hours will be the last hours of happiness in your pathetic life.

The description of this day is one for the Harlequin shelves.

I awoke early that morning, with the knowledge that she would be gone from my life by nightfall. Her musky scent was still on my pillow from the night before, bringing rise to my desire again early this morning. I rolled over and there she was. I saw it clearly then — she wanted me just as much as I wanted her — and somehow she knew it was all coming to an end.

I showered alone, feeling that even those brief 10 minutes away from her were too long.

We would spend our last day together visiting all the familiar places we had gone before, during our earlier days together — the park, the corner bar (outdoor patio, of course, because she had been banned from going inside a few years ago), and my car. Every kiss that day lingered ever longer. I had never held her tighter or with more love than I did as the sun began to set on our last day together.

Sometime just before midnight, we retired to my bed.

She would be gone by morning.

I had already removed most traces of her from the other parts of the house. This act was my feeble attempt to deflect some of the pain I knew would burst forth come the morrow.

The very depths of my wounded soul already longed for just one more day. My inner being was pulsing with a sad but wonderful contradiction of bittersweet longing, and hope for a new future without her.

I looked at her, I caressed her, I held her and watched her come alight beneath my hand. I knew I could touch her the way she wanted to be touched. The unspoken nuances of our relationship had taken 34 years to create, build, and nurture. Of course, I knew what she wanted.

Just as she had become a vital part of every breath I took; she knew the difference between the moments I merely wanted her company, and the moments when having her with me would give me solace or energy. She knew I often craved her, felt an insatiable need for her.

TAINTED LOVE

How would I survive without the very breath I had counted on every day for so many years?

Ours was a happy life, but its time had come to an end.

That last kiss was deep, meaningful. As I tried to pull her inside me to my core, where I hoped she could hide and stay forever, I knew it was over. There was nothing left but the ashes, the remnants of what was, a dying ember, and her taste on my lips.

Sated, if only for a moment, I rolled over, holding my pillow close and my emotions closer.

Her scent eventually left the room as I passed fitfully into a dreamless slumber.

This marked the end of a lifetime with my soul mate.

Goodbye, my lover.

Now, my non-smoking friends — imagine going through this scenario EVERY SINGLE TIME YOU DECIDE TO QUIT!

EVERY BREATH YOU TAKE
THE POLICE

A few days before Q Minus Zero I started listening to the hypnosis CD that taught me to see the sunshine on a cloudy day (wow, another chapter title I missed using!).

The practice of taking two really deep breaths when feeling stressed has turned out to be very helpful to me. However, in the early days of Q + 2 to Q + 30, these deep breaths were more like hyperventilating and sucking in air, and there was nothing calming about that!

I set my quit date (Q minus Zero) for December 6. There was no significance to that date.

I tend to attempt to quit on a Monday morning so I can smoke my brains out and get all tanked up on the weekend before. The thinking is that you make yourself so sick and disgusted by your filthy vices that on quit date you want to 'start clean' on many levels.

That's the theory.

The reality was that on the weekend my greatest stress was figuring out what time to take my nap. There WAS no stress on the weekend.

By Monday at noon (Q +14 hours) my day was already becoming a series of mini-stresses. Let's also keep in mind that of those 14 smoke-free hours, eight of them were spent sleeping, so by noon it was really only six waking hours of detox.

"Tina, you wimp," you say. Oh yeah, you bet.

The first days in any attempts to quit are always surreal.

You attempt to fill what would normally be smoke times with work stuff, thumb twiddling, gum chewing, whatever keeps your mind off smoking.

The irony is that every replacement habit you use actually makes you put your mind back ON smoking.

For example, "I am going to chew this stick of gum like it has the Hope Diamond in the middle because if I don't, I will think of smoking. So I'll chew, not smoke. So instead of a nice, smooth, *Player's* white-filtered beauty between my ready lips, I would much rather feel the muscles in my jaw torture this piece of *Juicy Fruit* until it begs for mercy, seeking refuge between my cheek and gum."

Drinking water (only from a bottle or through a straw works for smoke replacement purposes) certainly made me feel full and made my mouth always feel cleaned out. But when you are drinking from that bottle INSTEAD of lighting a cigarette, you might as well put it in a brown paper bag and pull it out from under your coat because you WILL attack that bottle with your lips like a wino going after cough medicine.

I felt as though I walked around looking freakishly zombie-like.

Knowledge that this might have been elaborately concocted by my own imagination did not make it easier to deal with.

Regardless, it can't have looked pretty from the outside.

MESSAGE IN A BOTTLE
THE POLICE

I was lucky to have had some people rooting for me when I quit and they would ask me about my progress. Here are some excerpts of e-mail messages with Linda on Q + 2… keep in mind that she had quit the day before as well.

——— Original Message ———
From: Tina
Sent: Tuesday, December 07, 2004 12:16 PM
To: Linda
Subject: how are you

Oh my, this morning, partway through the reception breakfast I thought I was going to crawl out of my skin….shakes, body aches….finally got to my car and primal screamed for 5 minutes to shake the DTs…..I guess I never made it to 'hour 36' before….

I've decided I will spend some of my volunteer time lobbying to have 'nicotine detox centers' developed as part of the health care system....I find it ridiculous that if I was a heroin addict I would be comfortably locked away and dealing with my withdrawal without the other realities of life, like my job, my relationships, etc.

Instead, though it is the most addictive substance on earth, I am regarded with "Oh, you'll get over it, lots of people quit, get a grip," when I don't even want to SEE another soul... I want to be at home (or in a strange building with a bed and no responsibilities that require my thought process to be functioning) and SLEEPING until this feeling GOES AWAY!!!

So, how YOU doin'?

T.

From: Linda
Sent: Tuesday, December 07, 2004 12:57 PM
To: Tina
Subject: RE: how are you

I am freaked out now!
Did you buy a pack?

From: Tina
Sent: Tuesday, December 07, 2004 1:20 PM
To: Linda
Subject: RE: how are you

No, it's almost passed…heading into a meeting….gonna go home after work and straight into bed I think…(feel like I'm going deaf and having a heart attack!)
Grrrr… almost over….

I also had some fun correspondence with others that unfortunately I didn't find record of (they likely had some foul language and were deleted by my I.S. server!).

CHURCH OF THE POISON MIND
CULTURE CLUB

Q + 3 was a day that began relatively well, all things considered. I had a totally disgusting cup of coffee, unaccompanied by a cigarette, had an uneventful drive into work, again unaccompanied by the usual three cigarettes, and looked at my 'affirmation card' about every 30 minutes.

As the afternoon progressed, however, I could actually feel a buzzing in my ears and my eyes began to take on that glazed 'deer caught in the headlights' look.

If you can imagine how a junkie looks when he's jones-ing for a fix — that was me by five o'clock.

My only thought was that I had to get home, feed the cats and go straight to bed and sleep (because frankly that is the ONLY time I am not thinking about smoking!).

TAINTED LOVE

I walked in the door and four cats swarmed me, climbed my legs, rubbed fur all over my newly dry cleaned pants and squealed like I had left them abandoned for a week. I could barely make it to the cupboard to get the tuna and bowls.

Don't get me wrong — the above description is the *typical* day arriving home — but on Q + 3, it was interpreted in my mind as follows:

MEOW, meow, MEOW, MEOW, meowwww, meeeooww, meowow, MEOW, meowow, MEOW, meow, MEOW, MEOW, meowwww, meeeooww, meowow!

Charlie: "Yo, woman, I've finished tearing up that carpet I love upstairs and I've worked up an appetite — how 'bout some grub?"
Simba: "I loosened all this orange fur so I can put it all over your clean black pants. Where you going? Come here, I've only rubbed one leg so far!"
Phantom: "What ever happened to ladies first? I am so tired of getting chased around by the boys — why can't you just get rid of them?"
Chester: "I know I'm new here but I can only hope she ain't gonna take her time like this feeding us EVERY night!"

In the time it took for me to remove my shoes, put down my bag and head upstairs to undress, they had already inhaled their food and were following me from room to room screaming for whatever else was on their minds:

MEOW, meow, MEOW, MEOW, meowwww, meeeooww, meowow, MEOW, meowow, MEOW, meow, MEOW, meowwww, meeeooww, meowow!

Simba: "Are you gonna let me out? How 'bout just in the garage, then, just for a couple minutes? I know, I'll stand on my hind legs and jog against the patio door for 20 minutes until you let me out."
Chester: "I've been hangin' around nothing but old farts all day. How 'bout a little fun? You know, chase a fake mouse or something?"
Phantom: "I love you so much that I am going to keep following you and meowing at you until you kiss me and pet me and love me back."
Charlie: "That Phantom is such a kiss-ass — I think I'll bite her."

TAINTED LOVE

Within about 30 minutes of this, in a slow crescendo I performed a mental swan dive where I envisioned myself throwing cats out the window or flushing them down the toilet.

I quickly realized that these were not rational visions and locked myself in the bathroom where the final thread holding the pieces of my mind together SNAPPED.

ALL CRIED OUT
LISA LISA AND CULT JAM

I started out by yelling at the cats through the door, "&#^#&^%**&^&^%$@*!!" And when that seemed to make them talk back louder I started to swear at them, "&^$#&@#$*!1 @#$%$#$#*^%$$%$#^^%!!*".

"I... C-A-N-T... T-A-K-E...I-T...A-N-Y-M-O-R-E...!!!"

At this point I shrank into one of the most pathetic poses known to woman (you know it — the one where you are sitting on a toilet seat, elbows on knees, head in hands — the Thinker pose for girls).

The sobs that came forth were straight out of the diaphragm. I could barely catch my breath between my staccato gasps. I might have laughed at the drama-queen sound of it all if it weren't for the fact that hearing myself laugh through that would likely have sent me into a state worthy of a rubber room and long-long-long-sleeved white jacket.

I wouldn't have thought it possible, but just like I had when I was a tot, I actually cried myself out. I was so physically drained after about 30 minutes of wailing that I barely had the energy to open the bathroom door to let myself out.

The interesting part of this was that I still had an unopened pack of cigarettes in my car downstairs this entire time. I knew it was there but I didn't go get it.

I recall somewhere in the deepest recesses of my mind calling Linda's cell phone to ask her not to call when she was on her way home because I was going to sleep. It likely sounded like this: "Sob **&%^ …*(&%@## bad day… $$#^&&&*!!!! ….don't call…..&*^*&&^%^%#@@ must kill the cats *&^*&%&$%#!!!"

She told me afterwards that the frantic message made her think I had started smoking again – NOT THAT I HAD SNAPPED MY MIND LIKE A TWIG, NOT THAT I NEEDED EMOTIONAL HELP, NOT THAT I AND EVERY LIVING CREATURE AROUND ME WAS IN IMMINENT DANGER! She thought the WORST! She thought I had started smoking again!

Hmmmpphh!

THAT'S WHAT FRIENDS ARE FOR
DIONNE WARWICK

It was at this mind-snapping-like-a-sugar-pea moment that Deb called. Everyone needs a friend like Deb. I am fortunate to have in my circle of life a group of about a dozen girls who have known each other from high school and earlier and Deb goes back to about grade 4. Didn't actually like her (and vice versa) until grade 7, but other than that, we've been the greatest of friends ever since.

My first forays into smoking were with Deb, way back when. Deb's Q minus Zero was more than 2 years ago (we were both supposed to quit that day. I failed, she succeeded).

When it was Deb on the other end of the line, I knew there was a Buddha. There are people you encounter in the process of quitting who give you advice, platitudes, rhetoric and stories of the people THEY know and how THEY succeeded in quitting.

Although you'll truly want to believe them, there's a small piece of your brain that internally yells "LIAR," or "YOU JUST WANT ME TO BE LIKE YOU," "LET'S MAKE EVERYONE SUFFER" and "CONSPIRACY!"

I knew that whatever Deb told me to be true, would be true – no holds barred.

I can't remember all that she said or how she said it, but I do know that she gave me examples of the against-all-odds successes I've had in my life, moments when I showed great resolve, and she even told me that when she had one of these 'brain snap' moments early in the quitting process, I had called her and helped her through it. I wasn't aware of this fact.

Though everyone tells you it gets easier the longer you hang in there, hearing it from Deb made it a reality for me… *if only I could hang in there until the 'easy time' came.*

When I hung up the phone from talking to Deb, I pulled on my flannel jammies, curled under the duvet and in a dream-like state, stared out the window with utter exhaustion, and then fell asleep.

If anyone had seen me at that moment before sleep, they might have glimpsed what strangely looked like I was sucking my thumb. Others may have seen it as the posture of holding a cigarette.

Regardless of how it looked, I had made it through another day.

WITCHY WOMAN
THE EAGLES

On my way home from work on Q + 7, I got a flat tire about three blocks from home at around 7:30 p.m..

I was destined on this very night to become Linda Blair's head-spinning *Exorcist* body double.

I smelled of fear and loathing, and the distance to walk home in one direction was about the same as the distance to walk to a store — and ultimately cigarettes — in the opposite direction.

I considered the flat tire to be a karmic test, one that I would surely pass with flying colors — I just had to stay calm.

First, I called the auto club where the on-hold message said that due to the frigid cold temperatures, they were experiencing a "higher than average volume of calls" and the wait would be at least

TAINTED LOVE

30 minutes. I could live with that. I'm good, I'm smoke free, and proud to be a virgin non-smoker (NOT a non-smoking virgin, which is ENTIRELY different!)

When a living person came on the line, I was informed that my membership of 20 years had expired six months earlier and that it would cost me $150 to renew on the spot. I did, and I'm still OK and still smoke free. She said I could expect someone in 30 minutes.

While I calmly waited the 30 minutes, I called my car dealer to inform them that my car would be brought in, and called home to say, "I'm OK, will be late, don't wait on dinner and, no, I'm not smoking." My karmic test was, thus far, a success.

Thirty-one minutes later, I called the auto club to let them know my new cell number, which I was pretty sure they didn't have. They said my guy was just around the corner, likely to be another five or 10 minutes. I said thank you, and that was the last nice thing I said on 'Day Q + 7.'

The actual wait time was two hours and 45 minutes and I never did find out the real reason for the excruciating delay.

Knowing that I could have walked home in three minutes and had them call me when they were at my car did not make each passing minute more bearable.

Knowing that dinner would not be happening at all tonight didn't help when all my fixations these days were oral.

I felt that I was blatantly lied to on repeated phone calls and that I would have been a sane person had someone actually told me it would be almost three hours of waiting — THEN at least I could have made other decisions!

Suffice it to say that the 16-year-old boy with the brand new auto club job was given a fast life lesson on the effects of withdrawal from drug addiction. With that lesson came the importance of changing a tire in 12 seconds, before the twitching lady pulls her own head off and hurls it at you.

To that young man who saw my lip quiver throughout my rant but kept a pleasant, nearly sympathetic demeanor, I apologize.

To Linda, who saw and heard the geyser erupt when I did eventually get home on three tires and a donut, I also apologize.

TURN BACK THE CLOCK
JOHNNY HATES JAZZ

This entire chapter should be done as an UM.

> *UM*
> Isn't EVERY book written in journal-like style really an UM?

When I was editing this book, I realized that there was a blank, non-existent period — a two week black hole of sorts.

The period between Q + 7 days and Q + 21 days is when my alter ego took over.

I have virtually no recollection other than to know deep in my gut that I was not aware of myself, and that I was likely unkind and confused.

I would have offered to have Linda or my co-workers, or anyone who saw me regularly at that fateful time, write this chapter, but I prefer to keep this book G-rated (and frankly, as positive a public account of ME as possible under the circumstances).

If I may relate what they might have been saying behind my back by using '80s song titles:

Beat It – Michael Jackson
Devil Inside – INXS
Animal – Def Leppard
Run Like Hell – Pink Floyd
Danger Zone – Kenny Loggins
Armegeddon It – Def Leppard
Don't Come Around Here No More – Tom Petty
Blasphemous Rumors – Depeche Mode
Cuts Like a Knife – Bryan Adams
Hazard – Richard Marx
I See Red – Split Enz
My Ever-Changing Moods – Style Council
Psycho Killer – Talking Heads

To those who spent any length of time with me in those blank two weeks, I hope this will pacify and subdue some of the anger.

And please, please stop letting the air out of my tires!

DO THEY KNOW IT'S CHRISTMAS?
BAND AID

Christmas was brutal.

What does every smoker want to do after a big meal? (*besides avoiding doing the dishes...*)

What does every smoker want to have along with their holiday cheer? (*besides an unlimited supply of salted jumbo cashews...*)

What does every smoker want to do when hangin' out with family? (*besides tuning out...*)

What does every smoker want to do on the one-hour drive on the way to hang out with family and on the one-hour drive BACK from hangin' with family? (*besides starving for turkey, then swearing that next year you won't eat so much...*)

A smoke. Mmmm….

Which is why Christmas was brutal! Torture, torture, torture….

For the first three weeks I DID feel I was sacrificing something I enjoy. This was totally counter to what the BOOK and my PLAN said I should be feeling.

I really DIDN'T want to quit, and it was ALL Linda's fault that I was even trying!

Just because SHE wants to quit and SHE thinks it's easier if I'm not smoking around her, SHE gets her way and ruins my life in the process.

OK, melodramatic but this was the start of the decline of my mental state and my first 'slip.'

When Kathy called from the other side of the country to say she would be in Ontario on a last-minute trip and was coming over for New Year's Eve, I saw my window of opportunity.

I could smoke with my smoking friend, just for a few days, thereby enjoying some holiday cheer as well, and generally be more pleasant to be around.

Linda, who pretty much felt the same withdrawal backlash, quickly agreed that we should take a wee sabbatical, with full intention to quit again on the Monday after the start of the New Year.

Simple really.

BACK IN THE HIGH LIFE AGAIN
STEVE WINWOOD

My mood swung like a saloon door.

I went from raving lunatic to doe-eyed fawn in one minute flat. Actually, in retrospect, I realize that just having made the decision that we would smoke resulted in the mood swing. It had little to do with the actual tobacco.

I spent most of that night paying little attention to my friends, or the new year celebration that I barely stayed awake for. It was all about the cigarettes.

I was on a four-day bender and nothing and nobody could stand in the way of this bliss.

I had a few early moments of nausea lighting up again, but I am strong-willed — I persevered until the nausea passed and changed shape, turning into rapt joy (this is where the sound of angels works well).

But like every good fall off the wagon, you know that just around the corner is the moment when you'll have to get back up and dust yourself off to join the real world again.

The real world meant having a *new* Q minus Zero.

After Christmas and New Year's Eve, I made an appointment to see my Reiki Master. I thought that perhaps my chakras were misaligned due to the two weeks of reducing my tar and nicotine counts, the month of not smoking, ongoing sinus infections, and a four-day smoking binge.

A little hands-on healing and I'd be back to my happy self.

I cried like a baby in that appointment.

I ranted like a lunatic about government conspiracy theories ("If it is that bad for you, they should just ban it altogether, instead of reaping the tax benefits — that's so hypocritical!").

I complained that Linda's a control freak and just wants me to quit as a tactic toward my submission.

I was subliminally (or NOT so subliminally) looking for somebody, ANYBODY to tell me it was OK to continue smoking.

Of the three-hour appointment, my mind will only let me remember one thing she suggested… that maybe a cigarette in my car once in a while wasn't such a bad thing.

YOU DON'T OWN ME
LESLEY GORE

> *UM*
> Yes, this is NOT an '80s song, but guess what? "*You Don't Own Me*" MAKES MY POINT! Write your OWN darn book!

There's a place in your own mentality where a sort of purgatory exists.

Heaven was where I would lounge on a beach under a warm sun and cool breeze having a cigarette... and all my friends were smoking too.

Hell was where I was a non-smoker surrounded by happy smokers who felt sorry for me for 'falling for the propaganda.'

Purgatory was where I convinced myself that I could straddle both worlds.

I spent the next two weeks smoking only in my car.

This action was justifiable as follows:
1. I am not smoking in front of Linda, nor telling her about it, thus I am not harming her chance of success in quitting smoking
2. I am not smoking around the general public, thus I am not emitting harmful second-hand smoke into the atmosphere
3. I will have a cigarette on my way in to work and on my way home — simple, everybody is happy in this scenario

The strangest thing about purgatory is that you desire to be either in heaven or hell instead. You really would prefer heaven but even hell is better from the purgatory point of view.

Sneaking around like this put an incredible mental strain on me.

Picture a devil on one shoulder and an angel on the other. They are bickering all day long, and worse, there is a ring of truth in what each of them says. You are meant to step in and pick a side but you can't because you are the consummate fence sitter. You know that life is all about the gray area, it's NOT black and white at all.

Internal conflict is the name of the game for a smoker trying to quit.

More often than not, I was thinking up reasons to give up trying to quit:

- I'm bitchy
- I'm gaining weight
- It's nobody else's business if I want to smoke

- I have no health issues so it's not like it's making me sick
- I've smoked for most of my life, so what's another 20 years of smoking going to do to me that wouldn't have already happened?
- There's no way in the world that they will ban smoking completely because of the $800 million in tax revenue that the government collects, so although it's socially unacceptable, I will always be able to buy cigarettes if I want to go back to smoking. Yeah, that's right, just me and my smoking friends, the only steadfast smokers left

It's not accidental that each of the reasons got longer as the list grew.

It's like lying. When someone asks you a question and you are going to lie in answer, you never give a short answer — you will always blabber, you can't help yourself.

As you can probably predict, the two cigarettes a day in my car began to increase, then spread to the garage. Then there was the subsequent division of the two cigarettes into six trips, smoking one third in each visit. Ah yes, and rather than smoking icky, re-lit smokes, I could just have three or four cigarettes, and so on, and so on… You know where this is going.

I could not survive as a part-time smoker. Purgatory would not work for me. I needed help deciding on heaven or hell.

IT'S THE END OF THE WORLD AS WE KNOW IT REM

"I think that perhaps your body has become used to the tar, nicotine, benzene, formaldehyde and other carcinogens it has ingested for the past 30-some-odd years and by giving up cigarettes, you are actually making your body sicker. I may have been wrong encouraging you to quit smoking, so I suggest you revert to smoking a pack a day for the good of your overall health."

This was the statement I had HOPED would come from my doctor's lips.

Since cutting down my smoking almost two months earlier, I had been plagued with a sinus infection that wouldn't go away, a dry, hacking cough that woke me every night, and grinding of my teeth and lip-biting in a very obsessive/compulsive manner — just a few of my new physical concerns.

TAINTED LOVE

In retrospect, I spent the first part of my life expecting to be long gone before any ill-effects of my actions caught up to me. Examples...

"I need not exercise because it's the 70 year olds who get arthritis and I don't intend to live that long."

"Eating well is silly because I have a very active metabolism and I'm small boned so weight gain will never be an issue."

> **UM**
> In my world, my metabolism also turns *Kraft Dinner* into high fiber granola.

> **UM**
> Wrinkles give me character and show that I smile a lot in life – and that's a good thing right?!

"I can sunbathe for hours wearing baby oil because Vitamin D from the sun is valuable."

"By smoking, I am keeping the stress at bay, ergo, my blood pressure is kept low and I won't have a heart attack."

"They say that a glass of wine a day is good for you and it's only a matter of time before they determine the same benefits from, say, Corona, or Kahlua, or Baileys — I'm actually just ahead of my own time."

So you can see how in my world of justifying my actions to fit my desires, I dreamed that my doctor would tell me that all my woes would be solved if only I would start smoking again.

Instead, the ever-thorough Dr. K. spent a good 40 minutes asking me questions about my successes, failures, ups and downs in the previous two months, then dutifully wrote the prescription, which looked like this:

The translation from 'doctor's-hand' to layman was:
nasal spray
cough suppressant, and
10 mg. of Prozac!!!

MOTHER'S LITTLE HELPER
ROLLING STONES

PHARMACY
Presents
Patient/Medical Information for….
TRIANO, Tina
For
PROZAC 10 mg.

---

(1) Fluoxetine - <u>ORAL</u> (flew-OX-eh-teen)

USES: Fluoxetine is a selective serotonin reuptake inhibitor (SSRI) used to depression, obsessive-compulsive disorder, panic attacks, certain eating disorders (bulimia), and a severe form of premenstrual syndrome (premenstrual dysphoric disorder (or PMDD). This medication works by restoring the balance of natural substances (neurotransmitters) in the brain, thereby improving mood and feelings of well-being.

1. Please don't make me imagine what an anti-depressant would be doing as anything BUT oral medication. Far be it from me to assume that a person with extreme anxiety is gonna fiddle with a suppository!

MOTHER'S LITTLE HELPER

OTHER USES: This drug is also used to treat certain other eating disorders (anorexia nervosa), obesity, and depression associated with bipolar disorder.

HOW TO USE: Take this medication by mouth usually once a day in the morning, with or without food, or as directed by your doctor. If your doctor tells you to take this medication, take a dose in the morning and at noon. Dosage is based on your medical condition and response to therapy. Use this medication regularly in order to get the most benefit from it. Remember to use it at the same time(s) each day. It is important to continue taking this medication even if you feel well. Do not stop taking this medication without consulting your doctor. Do not take less or more medication than prescribed. The maximum recommended dose for adults treated for obsessive-compulsive disorder and premenstrual dysphoric disorder is 80 mg. per day. The maximum recommended dose for children with attention-deficit hyperactivity disorder (ADHD) treated for depression is 20 mg. per day. It may takes 4 weeks or longer before the full benefit of this drug takes effect. Inform your doctor if your condition persists or worsens.

SIDE EFFECTS: Nausea, loss of appetite, diarrhea, dry mouth, trouble sleeping, dizziness, drowsiness, yawning, weakness or sweating may occur. If any of these effects persist or worsen, notify your doctor or pharmacist promptly. Tell your doctor immediately if any of these serious side effects occur: <u>unusual or severe mental/mood changes</u> (eg. Anxiety/mania), weight loss, change in sexual (2) desire and ability, vision changes. Tell your doctor immediately if any of these unlikely but serious side effects occur: uncontrolled movements (tremors), fever/flu-like symptoms. Tell your doctor immediately if any of these highly unlikely but very serious side effects occur: unusual muscle stiffness, fast/irregular heartbeats, chest pain, black stools, <u>vomit that looks like coffee grounds</u>, easy bruising/bleeding, unusual bleeding, seizures. (3)

2. Let my doctor know if this medication causes "unusual or severe mental/mood changes"? Correct me if I'm wrong, but isn't that WHY I'm taking this medication? …This is now a 'chicken and egg' scenario?
3. And SMOKING is BAD FOR ME?!

TAINTED LOVE

For males, in the very unlikely event you have <u>a (4) painful, prolonged erection (lasting more than 4 hours</u>), stop using this drug and seek immediate medical attention or permanent problems could occur. A serious allergic reaction to this drug is unlikely, but seek immediate medical attention if it occurs. Symptoms of a serious allergic reaction include: rash, itching, swelling, severe dizziness, trouble breathing. If you notice other effects not listed above, contact your doctor or pharmacist.

PRECAUTIONS: Before taking fluoxetine, tell your doctor or pharmacist if you are allergic to it; or if you have any other allergies. Before using this medication tell your doctor or pharmacist your medical history, especially of: liver disease, kidney disease, stomach bleeding, diabetes, seizure disorder. Though uncommon, depression can lead to thoughts or attempts of suicide. Tell your doctor immediately if you have any suicidal thoughts, worsening depression, or any other mental/mood changes (5) (including new or worsening <u>anxiety, agitation, panic attacks, trouble sleeping, irritability, hostile/angry feelings</u>, impulsive actions, severe restlessness, rapid speech). Keep all medical appointments so your healthcare professional can monitor your progress closely and adjust/change your medication if needed. If you have diabetes, fluoxetine may affect your blood glucose levels. Monitor your blood glucose regularly, and share the results with your doctor. The dose of your anti-diabetic medication(s) may need to be adjusted. Liquid preparations for this product may contain sugar and/or small amounts of alcohol. Ask your doctor or pharmacist about the safe use of this product if you have diabetes. This drug may make you dizzy or drowsy: <u>use caution when engaging in activities requiring alertness such as (6) driving</u> or using machinery. Limit alcoholic beverages. Caution is advised when using this drug in the elderly because they may be more sensitive to its effects, especially drowsiness. This medication should be used only when clearly needed during pregnancy. Discuss the risks and benefits with your doctor. If this medication is used during the last 3 months of pregnancy, infrequently your newborn may develop symptoms including feeding or breathing difficulties, seizures, muscle stiffness, jitteriness or constant crying. However, do not stop taking this medication unless your doctor directs you to do so. Report any such symptoms to your doctor promptly. Fluoxetine passes into breast milk and may have undesirable effects on a nursing infant.

```
Therefore, breast-feeding while taking this drug is not
recommended. Consult your doctor before breast-feeding.
```

4. Are men even aware that this drug is available?!
5. Ditto statement #2…
6. So let me get this straight… I am to take this pill every morning as soon as I open my eyes so that I can get through my day, which really shouldn't include turning on my coffee maker, driving my car to work, or turning on my computer once I get there?

I sum up this chapter with my mantra from this particular period in my life: I WAS NORMAL WHEN I WAS A SMOKER!

SECOND CHANCE
38 SPECIAL

Speaking of NORMAL, it's funny how years ago when I was taking an anti-depressant that was promoted as a smoking cessation drug, I felt no stigma about mental illness.

Now that I was on an anti-depressant as a direct result of my specific complaints about inappropriate reactions to life around me, as a RESULT of smoking cessation, it became a statement about my person.

I was prescribed two pills (20 mg.) per day to start and it was my mission in life to get that cut down to 10 mg. as soon as possible. Why? It was only because of my misguided sense of weakness that I was being medicated for 'mental instability' at all!

Alternately, during my earlier stint with that other brand of anti-depressant, I continued taking the pills even when my body was making it very clear that I should stop. Something about the annoying rash that covered ever square inch of my back, neck and ass should have offered me a clue. But there was no stigma, so I blamed the rash on a reaction to the sun, took daily oatmeal baths and continued poisoning myself in the attempt to quit smoking.

Thinking back to this irony makes me less rushed to get off the Prozac today.

And the whole "how many days has it been since you smoked" thing! Ugghh. If you do the math throughout this book, you will realize that I did NOT start all over again with a new Q + 1 when I faltered in late December and early January, SO SUE ME!

Frankly, and anyone who has 'slipped' will attest to this, if I were required, by royal decree of the land, to proceed to GO, NOT collect $200, and start at Q+1 AGAIN in my quit smoking effort, I WOULD STILL BE SMOKING TODAY!

I could not handle another failure.

Sure, some might say I cheated. I think I'm at month ten, but I'm really at month 8 ? and so on, but guess what? I didn't win any contests by quitting, I did actually continue saving money I did NOT spend on cigarettes (other than probably one rogue pack during the 'dark' time), so BITE ME!

OK, that might have been a little crass. Please accept my sincere apology.

TAINTED LOVE

The mind-bending concepts that run through a smoker's/ex-smoker's mind are frequent.

I used to think that EX-smokers were the most obnoxious creatures on the planet, spouting their holier-than-thou platitudes about what a filthy habit it is and how much better they feel now, blah, blah, blahdi-blah….

Having BECOME one of those creatures (though much less irritating, I hope!), I realize all those platitudes are like a self-brainwashing recording.

There is a deeply inherent fear in someone who has recently quit smoking that they will have gone through this extreme anguish for nothing. They KNOW they are only one smoke, one deep drag in fact, from going back to something they really didn't feel passionate about giving up in the first place. In retrospect, half a year away from the worst of the anguish, I often wonder why I quit.

Linda is much more confident than I am about her ability not to go back 'to the dark side.' She still loiters in purgatory because she likes to have a smoke or two when she's having a cocktail with smoking friends. It will likely only amount to a pack a year, which still beats a pack a day.

The 'poor me' side of my brain (or heart, perhaps) thinks that because she knows more than any one person just how difficult this process has been for me, it's mean for her to smoke at all.

So I've started sprinkling Prozac on her Corn Flakes.

Don't worry, my doctor says that Prozac can curb the appetite, and I'm sure she agrees that we could lose a pound or two of our 'quittin'-fat.'

I have always preferred drugs to real exercise anyway!

HURTS SO GOOD
JOHN COUGAR

When I started my third Q Minus Zero at the beginning of February, I decided that I should start working out. Not only would this be a new way for me to release all that nervous tension and keep my hands and mind busy after work, but it would keep me from gaining that incredible 'metabolism is slowing' weight gain.

I had a few things against me from the start of this activity.

First, I am a weakling.

Actually, let's be honest and cut right to the chase. Physically, I am a lazy bum. I have no desire to walk if I can drive, ride a bike if I can be transported by rickshaw or move AT ALL if I can just lie down and nap instead.

However, I do like the look of a body that's 'cut,' so that was my motivator.

Second, I am short and small boned by nature, standing a whole five foot two inches tall. In my early twenties I was 105 pounds, in my late twenties (what I call the I LOVE KAHLUA JUST A BIT TOO MUCH years) I ballooned to 130 pounds. Most frightening of all was that I had the extra weight on for some time, but just didn't realize it until I saw a photograph of myself in a tight pair of sweatpants, from a side profile. I was pitiful.

And I know there are truly overweight people out there saying I'm a suck and they would give their right leg to HAVE a right leg weigh 130 pounds, but you need the perspective. I had increased my body weight by 25%! I stopped drinking Kahlua and milk and immediately lost 10 pounds. I never lost my thighs completely, and hovered between 110 and 115 throughout my thirties.

Then I hit my early forties (where I think I'll stay awhile), and my body shape changed — the sand in my hourglass figure changed so that most of my sand was now in my belly, ass and thighs. I was becoming virtually devoid of sand in my bosom or my upper arms.

So weightlifting seemed the perfect thing for me.

THE PLAN was to weight lift one night, then walk a mile on the treadmill the alternate night. Linda would be on the alternating equipment each night, we would eat many salads and be 'cut' in no time.

TAINTED LOVE

In the first week I went from 117 pounds down to 112 pounds – SUCCESS!

In that first week I also decided that walking was boring, that my muscles were near atrophy for conditioning, and maybe Wonder Bread isn't actually considered "God's food" to anyone but me.

Have you ever seen a guitar string snap? P-I-N-G-G-G.

The entire exercise thing reminded me of a bike ride I had taken in the Cayman Islands with Linda about nine years earlier. I, of course, wanted to rent the mopeds to tour the seven-mile coast. Linda, whose mantra is: "I coulda been on the women's Olympic hockey team if they had one back then," insisted that I could handle it. We rode to Hell and back, and that's not just a term of endearment. There is actually a tourist attraction with weird black rock and 'the post office from Hell' to buy postcards and souvenir chachkas. I had actually thought it was a doable trip on the way there, when I didn't realize it was because the strong coastal wind was at my back.

On the return, however, it took about 15 seconds before I realized that as hard as my little legs pumped, I was going nowhere fast.

That's when I heard, for the first but not last time in my life, the P-I-N-G-G-G of a hamstring pulling.

Back to the present… Q + 3 months.

Thanks to the spiffy new scale Linda bought that actually measures body fat too, I was now back up to 120 pounds and 24% body fat. WHAT THE @&%$??!!

Just yesterday I heard those disgusting condescending words I've heard myself say to Linda when I wanted her to feel better about herself: "That's because muscle weighs more than fat."

Phoo-ey.

THE RIDDLE
NICK KERSHAW

Dr. K. also prescribed an exercise book. Not the physical kind of exercise, but a self-help book so I could answer questions and write them down in the book as an exercise toward self-analysis.

Working with this book was like having Dr. Phil sitting beside me all day pointing out irritating nuances about my psyche.

It's interesting when we do this sort of activity that we want to be likeable, even to ourselves. I approached this book and these exercises like the solving of a riddle. It would make ME more clear to ME.

It would also perhaps confirm for me that I am as close to perfect as humanly possible, and a little tweak here and there would bring my moods back into the level-headedness I had always boasted.

I felt quite raw and exposed during this period. Close your eyes and imagine if you will that it's late fall or early spring. You are out for a drive in a neighborhood in which you have driven on numerous occasions. Except that it is at *this* moment that you see it — a house where you didn't even know one existed, with no leaves on the trees to obstruct the view, you can see it. At any other time of year you merely drive past a grove of trees, but now you know it exists and so you pull over and gaze at it for the first time.

It's possible that you'll see a nice house, but there's always a chance you'll see a shack and think, "Wow, isn't it a good thing we can't see that ugly shack all year round?"

Quitting smoking stripped away what I saw as my protection — my leaves had camouflaged what I feared would be a shack underneath it all.

As it turned out, my shack was a bit of a fixer-upper, and all I needed were the right tools.

According to the book, it was important to the process of mood identification to change your "automatic" thinking to "balanced" thinking.

Example:
Action: Linda tells me that I weigh more because muscle weighs more than fat.
Automatic Thinking: %#*%%&&!!!
Balanced Thinking: %#*%%&&!!!
Ok, so I skipped a chapter… Hang in there for a second and I'll be right back…

UM Good place for the *Final Jeopardy* music…

Now I got it, let's try that again....

The trick, as I just read in the missed chapter, is to actually find evidence to prove your automatic thoughts, then find evidence to disprove them, thus allowing you to have a balanced perspective.

So in the example above, the proof, in my mind at least, that she is a %%^#%#^**!!! might be: "she's jealous that I don't have to diet, because I'm not vain and I don't care about my weight," or "she's just plain old being snarky, that's why she says nasty stuff."

The disproving of the evidence might sound like: "she really does care about me and my health," or: "she noticed that I have made an effort to exercise and is impressed by how buff I've become."

The new result is a 'balanced' thought about the statement or 'action' that caused me to have a mood shift.

So now, with my new-found wisdom, the example might look like this:

Example:
Action: Linda tells me that I weigh more because muscle weighs more than fat.
Automatic Thinking: %#*%%&&!!!
Balanced Thinking: I realize that because Linda does not want to see me fail, she is protecting my feelings and thereby encouraging me to continue, oh and by the way — %#*%%&&!!!

Baby steps, my friends.

Chapters one through five in the exercise book made it clear that although outwardly I am a fairly happy and easy-going person, inside I am a screaming banshee when it comes to my own control issues.

I don't necessarily feel I need to be in control, but I DEFINITELY do NOT want anyone ELSE in control.

I'm OK with spontaneous activity that places NOBODY in control. But, I DEFINITELY do NOT want anyone ELSE in control.

If you feel you would LIKE me to be IN CONTROL, I can do that for you, just don't TELL me I HAVE TO be in control.

And if you RELINQUISH CONTROL to me, do NOT tell me in what way I should exert my control, as that's for ME to CONTROL, not YOU.

The response to these thoughts from my friend sitting beside me was always the same:

"And how's THAT workin' for you?"

It was time to put away the book.

POUR SOME SUGAR ON ME
DEF LEPPARD

There is one undisputable fact that all ex-smokers must admit: food tastes awesome now!

For the most part, I now find certain cheeses and gherkin pickles really strong tasting, but raspberries... mmm, make those little salivary glands behind my molars stand up and drool for more.

I discovered little breadsticks over the Christmas holidays and my breadsticks and I went everywhere together for a time.

Sugar has always been my weakness (my coffee is double cream & 5 sugars) but now I had blossomed into a full-fledged saccharin junkie.

My home and office had a regular stash of Tootsie Rolls, Werther's, Butter Rum Lifesavers, Nibs, Ju-Jubes, Jelly Bellies, Twizzlers, Lika-Maid, Pez, shoestring licorice, Passion Flakies, sponge 'just bring on the cavity' toffee, black licorice pipes and of course, candy cigarettes.

> *UM*
> I love to tie shoestring licorice into dozens of knots before eating it... mmm.

Six months into quitting, when I thought the worst was well behind me, I found myself doing the DQ drive-thru for a Raspberry Cheesequake Blizzard. It tastes like 4,000-some-odd calories delivered orally but plastered directly onto your inner thigh within moments of swallowing. This was my new and improved stress-relieving nicotine replacement.

> *UM*
> Did you know that as a Blizzard Fan Club member, you see all the commercials FIRST? Cool!

I told a doctor at my hospital (conversationally, of course) about my fear and potential dilemma of porking out now that I had quit smoking. She informed me that I would have to gain 100 pounds to have the same negative effects on my body that were caused by smoking.

I have calculated that I could have a Cheesequake every day for the next seven years before it will get me that extra 100 pounds.

Bring it on, I say... and while we're at it, if there's anyone from DQ reading this, any chance you're looking for an honorary President of the Blizzard Fan Club? I yearn for the distinction.

And according to my new thighs, which for the first time in my life actually RUB TOGETHER when I'm walking, I've EARNED the distinction!

TAINTED LOVE

EAT IT
WEIRD AL YANKOVIC

It's ALL about food when you quit smoking, so here are the alternate Song Titles from the '80s that almost became chapter titles:

Knock(wurst) *Three Times* – Tony Orlando
Rock Lobster (Tails) – B52s
Angel (Food Cake) *of the Morning* – (Orange) Juice Newton
Back (Bacon) i*n Black* (Angus steak) – AC/DC
White Wedding (Cake) – Billy Idol
Boys(enberry) *of Summer* (Sausage) – Don Henley
Sugar Sugar – The Archies (no edit required!)
Buffalo (Wings) *Stance* – Neneh Cherry (Pie)
Heart and (Filet of) *Soul* – Huey Lewis & the News
Another Brick (of Cheese) i*n the Wall*(nuts) – Pink (Grapefruit) Floyd
Burnin' Down the House (Salad) – Talking Heads (of Lettuce)
Holding Out for a Hero (Sandwich) – Bonnie Tyler
Hot (Cross Buns) *in the City* – Billy Idol

TAINTED LOVE

I (Tuna) *Melt with You* – Modern English (Muffin)
(Alaskan) *King* (Crab) *of Pain* – The Police
(Hershey's) *Kiss on My List* – Darryl Hall & John (Toasted) Oates
Lean (Cuisine) *on Me* – Club (Sandwich) Nouveau
Raspberry (Cheesecake) *Beret* – Prince
Let My Love Open the Door (To the Oven) – Pete Townsend
Live it Up (Side-down Cake) – Mental as Anything
(Chocolate Milk) *Shake it Up* – The Cars
Pump Up the (Strawberry) *Jam* – Technotronic
Puttin' on the Ritz (Crackers) – Taco
Radio Free (Range Chicken) *Europe* – REM
(Rocky) *Road* (Ice Cream) *to Nowhere* – Talking Heads
(Buttered) *Roll With It* – Steve Winwood
(Cool) *Whip It* – Devo

And just in case you don't think I came up with enough of these, I will add just one more that was provided in the comments that came back from my editor, Tara Mathey from Australia. She said she just couldn't help herself –

Nutbush City Limits – Tuna Turner

Let us bow our heads and give thanks — I made it past the 2nd month. Can somebody pass me the cranberries?

DANGER ZONE
KENNY LOGGINS

Have you noticed how many people wear a patch now?

It seemed only a decade ago when I could say I was on 'the patch' and that meant I was quitting smoking.

Now it might be assumed I was having delivered any or all of the following trans-dermally:

- estrogen
- pain medication
- testosterone
- Attention Deficit Disorder medication
- nutrients (though apparently this is still a decade away)
- progesterone
- electrolysis

Knowing that I might actually need more than one of these items at the same time frightens me.

As the quitters know, you must ensure that you don't place the patch on the same area of skin within a few days of each other.

I'm not sure if it's because the skin could break out in a rash from the glue on the patch, or because the drugs thin your skin and make the meds more easily transderm-ed, or because some people like the feeling of tiny hairs being RIPPED off of strange body parts.

And the gradually decreasing milligrams of nicotine actually DO exist for a reason. The plan, for you non-smokers, is to start with a 21 milligram patch if you smoke a lot, then after a week or so go down to 14 milligrams, then 7, then you will have gradually weaned yourself off of nicotine.

My Patch Experience (or Math for Dummies):

21 milligrams X 21 days = I'm happy, though possibly running out of body parts to stick.

Followed by:

0 milligrams X 2 days = proud of myself, though I slept through much of it.

Add being back to work on Monday and:

21 milligrams X 4 hours after the 2 days X 0 milligrams = nicotine overdose, multiplied by vomiting into a bag while sitting in my car at the side of the highway.

Next time, I'll stick with the electrolysis patch!

VIDEO KILLED THE RADIO STAR
THE BUGGLES

I'm a rock legend.

No really, I am.

There's a point in one of my past lives (perhaps a future life) where I am sure to have been a soulful Queen Latifah or Aretha Franklin.

Don't let the fact that I am a short white girl with a voice whose best, possibly only, good key is that of the Carpenters, Anne Murray and strangely Roch Voisine, fool ya.

> *UM*
> If you listen really close, Karen Carpenter and Roch Voisine sound exactly the same... he began his career when she died... hmmm.

Anyhow, I do like to sing, much to the chagrin of everyone close to me. Let me take this opportunity to apologize to my neighbors for the summer nights with my windows open. Most notably,

TAINTED LOVE

I need to apologize for the condition of my voice (or perhaps how I HEAR my voice), since Q Minus Zero.

Perhaps it's the minimal use of alcohol since then, or that my throat has lost its husky, Kathleen Turner/Janis Joplin/*some would say Keith Richards* quality since the elimination of tobacco, but my rock star self seems to be slipping away.

My karaoke machine sits idle now, her tangle of microphone cords splayed haphazardly, almost poetically, as though wishing to slither away to a more grateful home.

> *UM*
> I just flashed back to that IKEA commercial that makes you feel sorry for the lamp left at the curb! I LOVE that commercial.

Most of my singing now is practically under my breath. I don't belt it out for the world to hear. I no longer boldly sing in my car with the windows down at a stoplight. I fear that my confidence in my own singing is shaken.

Worse, just last week I caught myself humming to muzak in an elevator. Lord have mercy.

ALWAYS SOMETHING THERE TO REMIND ME   NAKED EYES

You can only avoid smokers and tempting situations for so long.

Now I have virtually no close friends who smoke, none of my colleagues in my office still smoke, and those I know who do smoke are not part of my regular routine. This was a good thing.

Vacationing in Cuba at the end of month three, as it turned out, was a bad thing.

Stepping off a plane into a smoke-filled airport was surreal.

I thought back over all the vacations I have taken in my life, where smoking had become increasingly prohibited.

Today in North America, you will find it difficult to find a hotel where they even HAVE smoking rooms. Some hotels have snitch lines where you can bust someone you see smoking on a BALCONY!

I have spent the last decade being catapulted kicking and screaming into a new non-smoking, militant anti-smoking era — like it or not.

Bars have all but placed a 'Do not enter — non-hazardous air inside' on the door. Patio bars have popped up every 10 feet and even some of those have become smoke-free.

At some point, just in the last five years I think, it's become socially unacceptable to be seen smoking in a car with a child inside.

And apparently, as I learned on this particular vacation, I have become somewhat comfortable with the new rules.

I arrived at the resort, stepping into a fog of Cuban cigars smoked freely in the lobby by men and women alike.

At dinner, I sat in the non-smoking section not 12 inches from the smoking section. Apparently there was an invisible barrier which precluded the exhaled smoke from meandering past it and into my own environment.

Flashback:

- I remember smoking in line at the bank as a girl in my teens
- In my twenties I smoked at my desk (my boss smoked cigars at his desk)
- I also smoked in an airplane, and yes —
- …I even smoked in a hospital room while visiting an ill friend!

Back to Castro-land, I spent my one-week vacation in Cuba with Linda and her parents (Momma Bear and Poppa Bear) testing my new limits as a non-smoker/ex-smoker/recovering smoker.

During this time I discovered all-you can-eat buffets alongside a family who specializes in food discussions as an Olympic sport. They have earned bronze medals in the 'where they ate and with whom they ate it' category, while netting a gold in the 2005 'what they ate, what they saw that they would never eat, and what they're gonna eat in a future meal' competition.

I learned that alcohol tastes better with a cigarette and therefore alcohol will need to be re-introduced later in the quitting process.

I also re-discovered lying in a rope hammock and napping with the sun on my face.

I remembered on this vacation how tasty water could be (bottled only, of course!) and how stinky cigars really are when you're exposed to them more often than just on special occasions.

And as I entered the plane to go home (having eaten a wonderful toasted cheese panini and discussed it thoroughly in the airport with my extended family), I actually craved my return to the comfort of the stifling conformist non-smoking world.

Who knew?

WHITER SHADE OF PALE
PROCOL HARUM

It seemed like a good idea at the time.

A great deal of thought went into determining what I would do with the boatload of money I would save by quitting. It got me through many moments to picture myself lounging on a beach or sleeping on top of a pile of $10 bills. It was difficult for me, however, to wait until I had saved enough for another vacation — I required an earlier reward.

My teeth have never been particularly white, and perhaps smoking for more than 30 years helped make them the dingy color they are. So it seemed like a smart idea to spend my first $500 saved by having my teeth professionally whitened. In my altered mind state, it was not only a good reward, but I figured I was likely not to yellow them again by smoking — so it was a good motivator all-around.

WHITER SHADE OF PALE

TAINTED LOVE

Perhaps it was being unaware of what actually takes place that was my first mistake.

I booked a treatment at a spa. I had visions of lounging around in a fluffy robe on a down-filled mattress with Enya playing in the background. In this perfect world, Heidi was also massaging my feet with peppermint lotion and Sven was rubbing my scalp until I fell asleep. While asleep, little angels painted my teeth with a lovely, minty, white cream (with a slight vanilla custard taste!).

When I awoke from this oasis, I would be handed a mirror to see my new sparkling teeth, but not before donning full UV protection sunglasses to ensure no cornea damage from such brightness! After a number of oohs and aahs from Heidi and Sven (and even Enya), I would arise from my feather bed, give my minions a royal wave over my shoulder, and ride off into the sunset to smile at all who passed by.

That was my vision; this was my reality:

I was on a gurney (no disrobing required — in fact, I still had my shoes on), something resembling steel dental floss was wedged into my gums beneath the teeth being treated, and a plastic gizmo was wedged into my mouth (and my lips tucked around it nicely) — all intended to keep my mouth open for an hour.

No Enya. No Heidi. No Sven.

For a frame of reference, let me inform you that I have spent the last 25 years of my life getting laughing gas in order to tolerate a teeth cleaning. I was now willingly allowing someone to put peroxide on my teeth, 'agitate it' every 15 minutes and place a light against them — and "oh, by the way, you may feel jolts of electricity going through your teeth" — and I was paying $500+ for the privilege! My top teeth were in such pain that I started to move my mouth so only the bottom teeth would get the light treatment for the last 15 minutes. Take a wild guess what THAT resulted in — yes, you guessed it: ultra-white bottom teeth, semi-white top teeth.

That entire night I was popping pain killers and squinting my eyes against the sudden bursts of pain going through the roots of my teeth, straight into my brain. This, I say, THIS, was my first reward for quitting smoking.

P.S. I found out three weeks later at my check-up at the dentist that I had a cavity in my right front tooth (brought on by the candy binges, exacerbated by the bleach). Someone needs a karma cleansing, don't you think?!

FIGHT FOR YOUR RIGHT TO PARTY
BEASTIE BOYS

I am on the fence still at month five.

On the left side of the fence I discuss smokers in the 'we.'

The right side of the fence says that if I've quit it should be 'they.'

They have just outlawed smoking on the property where I work, with the penalty of dismissal upon repeated non-conformance to the new policy.

> *UM*
> May I express that, ironically, now that folks are not allowed to smoke on the property, they smoke DIRECTLY OUTSIDE MY OFFICE WINDOW!

Left side: NANNY-STATE! Why are there people in power who have to control the lives and impulses of others?! Whatever happened to freedom for individuals? I should have the right to be stupid if I so choose, wear a motorcycle helmet or not, undo my seatbelt when I'm a block from my house — give me my freedom!

Right side: I work at a hospital that is a month away from opening a cancer centre where radiation and chemotherapy will be administered to thousands. If there's a place where smoking should be banned, this is certainly it.

Left side: Let's picture the woman as a patient in my hospital at the end of her life with meager hope and even fewer opportunities to do something that gives her pleasure. She smokes because there's little point in quitting now, and she'll be dragging her IV pole out to the street with her ass flapping in the winter wind because the bureaucrats think we should be one of the first smoke-free hospitals in the province.

Right side: the hospital is offering smoking cessation programs for that patient and if the patient whose ass is flapping on the street had had such help 10 years ago, she may not be at the end of her life today.

Frankly, those who know me would say I sit *directly on the fence* with barbed wire firmly planted on each butt cheek.

I was grateful to have quit *prior* to my knowledge of the proposed ban because I'm stubborn and frankly wouldn't have attempted to quit had I thought it was being legislated for me.

Deep in my gut I fight for the smoker's right to enjoy that cigarette and I secretly hope they don't give in to the 'establishment' and quit.

I believe that the government should just ban tobacco products all together, instead of nickel and dime-ing their hand-slapping gestures against tobacco — putting pictures of bad teeth on the pack, keeping cigarettes out of view, adding more and more 'sin' taxes. If they truly wanted it done with, they would forego the BILLIONS in taxes they generate and do the right thing by outlawing it. But they won't ban it, they'll just make it bloody uncomfortable for those who still smoke.

The east coast of Canada, from Quebec to the Atlantic provinces, has the highest concentration of smokers and they are the last to get on the non-smoking bandwagon. Often considered the smoking section of Canada, even they have placed 'stool pigeons' at bars to squeal on the covert smoker.

An era appears to be coming to an end.

There are moments when I wish I had been around throughout the '40s and '50s. Wally and I would be seen with our filterless *Pall Malls* and envied, and the non-smoker would be the minority. A girl can dream, can't she?

And somewhere deep in my heart of hearts, I hold out hope that some little bit of research, similar to the one that says a glass of red wine a day is good for you, will someday, perhaps in my lifetime, reveal that smoking really ISN'T bad for you, that there is no such thing as second-hand smoke, and it really was just our own polluted environment, monumental moments of stress, or mosquito bites that caused cancer all along.

WEIRD SCIENCE
OINGO BOINGO

As if by wishing, dreams could come true, the following is an actual newspaper headline six months into my non-smoking life:

> **"Smoking: An excellent way to prevent ulcers, reduce the risk of Parkinson's disease, relieve schizophrenia, boost your brain cells, speed up your thinking, improve your reactions and increase your working efficiency."**
>
> As appeared in *The Globe and Mail*

If you're a smoker seeing this article for the first time, refrain from the happy dance I caught myself doing when I read it.

I pictured myself making dozens of copies of the article and mailing them out to some key people:

First, one should be sent to my Dad. Dad has been mailing me 'reasons to quit smoking' articles all my life. ...Maybe I would laminate his copy.

This article confirmed what I've been saying all along — it's actually MORE HEALTHY for me to smoke!

But wait — let me save you the trouble of finding and reading the entire article, as there's a twist. To paraphrase, the article implies that the Chinese Government sells these health benefits as propaganda to Chinese citizens because the same government OWNS the tobacco industry. If the Chinese population quits smoking for health or other reasons, it could bankrupt the country.

Dang, I guess I'll keep waiting on the right research paper...

For every article you throw at a smoker to prove the perils of smoking, they can boomerang an equal and opposite statement of smoking benefits back atcha.

Forces International has a website that keeps track of the studies:

- You know the picture of the bad teeth and gums on a Canadian cigarette pack? Apparently, according to a Doctor's Guide Review from the *Journal of Periodontology*, "Smoking does not increase risk of receding gums."
- The *Orlando Sentinel* published an article that reported that a nicotine compound could combat tuberculosis.
- The National Library of Medicine published: "children of mothers who smoked at least 15 cigarettes a day tended to

have lower odds for suffering from allergic rhino-conjunctivitis, allergic asthma, atopic eczema and food allergy, compared to children of mothers who had never smoked."
- Carbon monoxide, a by-product of cigarette smoke, may alleviate heart attacks and stroke, according to an article published by a *HealthScout* reporter.
- Smoking (or nicotine) appears to be protective against arthritis, colorectal cancer, colitis, Tourette's Syndrome, and the list goes on....

Now, I don't expect the non-smoker to read these articles and say, "Gosh darn, we were wrong — we oughtta un-ban smoking!"

What I can hope for, however, is that they realize this:

Like everything else in life, if we could get off our high horses of black and white, we might find that there is a big fat gray area where we can live harmoniously as brothers and sisters of the same planet.

(End dream sequence; exit stage left.)

By the way, I only intend to quit until I'm 80 or on my deathbed — whichever comes first.

MELT WITH YOU
MODERN ENGLISH

On the subject of 80 years old…

At 43 years of age, I'm presently on the downhill side of being halfway there.

So this might, by some actuarial tables for the purpose of mortality rates, constitute middle age for me.

> *UM*
> Wasn't it only a few years ago that I was IN the '80s, dancing alongside my friends with their 'Flock of Seagulls' hair?! How can I possibly be middle-aged?

Middle-aged men get to have a mid-life 'crisis' that involves fast cars, faster women and a desire to dress younger than they are. You call that a CRISIS?!

Women get menopause — now THAT'S a crisis.

In my ninth month as an ex-smoker, it was confirmed by Dr. K. that I am peri-menopausal.

For the layman, peri-menopause means the beginning stages of menopause — sort of a trial run, warm-up, let's-practice-having-the-symptoms-of-menopause-but-without-the-upside-of-having-no-more-periods.

Some of the symptoms I had been experiencing in the previous 6 or 7 months I wrongly attributed to body changes in response to being smoke-free.

For example:

Insomnia – I had assumed it was a side effect of the Prozac.

Irregular periods – I assumed it was a combination of the stress of quitting and a side effect of a major change in my body's intake of nicotine.

Thickness in the middle – Cheesequakes… need I say more?

Hot flashes – It felt strangely like my earlier anxiety attacks. The night sweat version could just as easily have been a direct result of wearing flannel to bed.

The 'girls' and other signs of a girlish figure – my breasts, my entire body shape for that matter, has previously been on the boyish side. I chalked this new look up to 'retaining water and bloating' associated with missed periods and, again, Cheesequakes.

Finally, when my thoughts were clear enough to realize that all these symptoms, in addition to four months without a period, might mean a hormone change of some sort, I had the confirming blood test, which brings me to my current peri-menopausal diagnosis.

Dr. K. didn't suggest hormone replacement, much to my chagrin.

Instead, it was suggested that perhaps getting off my fat (sorry, girlish figure) ass and exercising was in order.

Dang it, who can find the time?

PATIENCE
GUNS N' ROSES

Time is something I have little of since Linda decided my 43rd birthday present would be slow insanity disguised as the hobby of *bonsai* (and no, I'm not really sure if the word is to be used as a noun, verb or adjective!)

I have *bonsai*-ed (trimmed excessively) a *bonsai* (small tree) while partaking in my new *bonsai* (art form) hobby.

She gave me NINE *bonsai* trees at various stages of *bonsai* (the verb).

Some of these trees had been nurtured to their current stage over a period of many years of loving care. My mission, should I choose to accept it, was to keep them alive through further generations.

And this was meant to re-direct my stress to create calm!

TAINTED LOVE

Talk about pressure!

I am methodical by nature, so I bought a book that same day (one with lots of pictures because I can't focus enough to read at length) and studied.

May I say, there are many reasons I chose not to have children.

They are likely the same reason I thought I would not like *bonsai*, and I now feel like I have nine children!

Let me introduce you to them:

The twins, Jason and Jimmy, appear to have the same daddy, with limbs branching out in all directions. They come from the juniper side of the family tree and already appear to be trouble-makers as they enter their teens and look to outgrow their pots before they're ready.

Fanny and Frances are the ficus sisters. With long hair requiring much trimming and some strengthening hair product, they are the divas of the group.

Little Jade and her older siblings Jasmine and Jebediah are the best-behaved children in my new family, and require the least attention. They are content to have just a moment's pampering and go back to their usual laidback position.

Although as a new parent I probably shouldn't pick one over the others, Jade really is my favorite.

The lineage of Biff and Betsy is questionable and lately I question if some riff-raff members of the dandelion family on the other side of the tracks ain't been messin' round my garden. I best be keepin' an eye out.

I'm tired lately.

With worrying about how my children will turn out constantly playing on my mind, it's a wonder I get any sleep at all.

My new children require:

Daily misting, thrice-weekly soil wetting, once-weekly water submerging, periodic root combing and replanting into ever more shallow bonsai pots, pinching of larger leaves, wiring of the branches to direct the growth into an acceptable design type (the ever popular semi cascade, for example), and the moisturizing of branch-cut areas with special lubricant.

At the time that I write this chapter, I have reached Q + 10 months, and Fanny appears to be in need of a paediatrician. Her hair has become dry and brittle and her siblings seem ashamed to be displayed on the same table with her. I tend to her physical and emotional needs but I fear the end is nigh.

I wonder if I would do any better with tobacco plants.

PAPA DON'T PREACH
MADONNA

On December 6th, I celebrated one year smoke-free (with the aforementioned couple of cheats early on!).

My work colleagues marked the occasion with a congratulatory card — it meant a lot to me that they knew how momentous an occasion it was in the grand scheme of my life's events.

I had discovered a great deal about my habit and my mental responses to stress and myself in general during the past year.

> *UM*
> In MY head this is sung to the tune of *These Are a Few of My Favorite Things…*

Water and books, then there's food and your good friends…
Exercise, self-help, celery sticks with Cheez Whiz.
Put it together and it leads you to snack…but you'll be OK cuz there's always Prozac!

My new attention deficit/obsessive-compulsive personality has resulted in some negative changes, and some positive ones.

So far, I've not been able to focus enough to finish reading a book…

…but on the bright side, I have WRITTEN one.

I forget entire conversations I just had, but I can remember movie numbers from the video store I worked at in the '80s (how freakishly *Rainman*).

I've found some cool websites, my favorite is www.stupid.ca.

This site was created by the Government and targets youth to quit smoking. I found the site after seeing a hilarious commercial showing a teenage girl rolling around in dog poop with the premise of 'Why would you make yourself stink on purpose?'

It's interactive and if you know a teen who smokes (or an adult with a teenage brain like mine), I highly recommend it.

I've had discoid lupus for the past nine years, the symptoms of which seem to be subsiding since I quit.

At a point in the fourth month I lit a cigarette and it not only tasted like crap, it felt foreign between my fingers. THAT was a big surprise to me. I had held a cigarette between my fingers every day, multiple times each day, for 35 years and now after four months it felt weird to do it.

TAINTED LOVE

That fact alone gives me hope as I pass the Q+ 11 month period.

People who have never smoked congratulate me for achieving my goal of quitting.

I am grateful for all the support around me, but I'm pretty sure they don't understand just what it meant to go through this. I write this account so that they will.

I believe I have an addictive personality, if there really is such a thing. I'm even more certain of it now that I have replaced smoking with new addictions — some might say healthier addictions — Cheesequake Blizzards and thumb drumming among them.

I am certain that those who have never had an addiction will never truly relate, though that's not to say that they can't be sympathetic. Obviously I had more non-smokers cheering me on than smokers!

Then there are the ex-smokers.

I run across people in my day who tell me that after 3, 5, 10 and even 25 years of having quit, they still get cravings.

I'm sure they mean well.

I guess they are saying what prompted me to write this book in the first place — it's *not* easy for everyone.

If you want to quit, you'll eventually get over the worst bits, but you'll never forget one of your first loves — as tainted a love as it may be.

I still have dreams in which I have to decide to smoke or not smoke; in more and more of theses dreams I now choose NOT to smoke.

Dig deep, use all the tools at your disposal. It will likely be a combination of things that will eventually work for you.

Eventually, my combination of tools this time around included (in this order):

Pre-Quit:
Self-Help Book #1, Hypnotism/Stress-Reduction CD

Month One:
Affirmation Cards, Candy, Water, ANY Food Product

Months Two & Three:
Prozac, Nicotine Patch & Self-Help Book #2

Months Four, Five & Six:
Prozac, Raspberry Cheesequake Blizzards

Months Seven to Eleven:
Prozac & realizing I will actually finish this book!

In essence, my success is clearly a result of the above tools, a warped sense of humor, a love of music and a support system of many wonderful people (and cats).

MEOW, meow, MEOW, MEOW, meowwww, meeeooww, meowow,

TAINTED LOVE

MEOW, meeeooww, meowow, MEOW, MEOW, meowwww, meeeooww, meowow!

Charlie: "Now when I bite you I don't get that icky taste of nicotine in my mouth."
Simba: "It's weird but my motility problem seems to have cleared up."
Chester: "Crazy you should say that, but my respiratory issues are gone too."
Phantom: "I love you so much I am going to keep following you and meowing at you until you kiss me and pet me and love me back" (some things never change).

And Phantom of course reminds me to make this important point to those of you thinking of quitting — if you don't quit just yet, you're still a valuable human being, and don't let anyone tell you otherwise!

But do keep in mind… **we ALL quit sooner or later — it's just a matter of being alive to see it happen!**

DRIVE
THE CARS

I have new-found money, energy and interests now.

My latest hobby is go-karting. Subliminally it may well be that I enjoy inhaling the gasoline fumes that sit at my right shoulder throughout the 20 laps. It also could be that I replaced a pointless, unending cycle of repetitive motion and behavior with another. Somehow it's virtually impossible to think about a smoke when you are flying down a track at 50 miles per hour wearing a fire-retardant racing suit, racing boots, racing gloves, neck brace, rib protector and 10-pound helmet with full-face visor. And did I mention the other 15 drivers who would just as soon see your back end spinning off the track into the tire pit, as they would smile and flip you the bird as they pass you?

Earlier in my life, during my 'lean' years, I drove a vehicle of a different kind and I was not only able to smoke, it was expected; those were the days — my cab-driving days....

Ah the memories...

Once the '80s ended, I was lost in a sea of Billy Ray Cyrus and Rick Astley. I mean, really — who could think straight in the early '90s under those conditions?

Finding myself between fundraising jobs, I thought I could take two of my favorite pastimes — driving and meeting new people — and make a job of it. I was in Niagara Falls, big tourist town, lots of fares — I thought I'd be rich. And considering I was living at the 'Y' at the time, these were happy thoughts.

The reality was that I got up at four a.m., cleaned the two feet of snow off my cab and then sat in it playing cards with fellow cabbies Mike, Norm and Bob while waiting for jobs that came six hours apart in a 12-hour day. I might have been bad at cab driving, but I rocked at euchre. And frankly, if any of us were in the middle of a winning streak, we would actually pass up one of our two daily calls! Ah those were the days... We all smoked, we each made $5 a day — just enough for a pack of cigarettes — and life was good.

But I digress... Back to the present, and go-karting.

I am not great... Well, if I'm being honest, I'm not even that good...

...Well, fine then... one of my racing mates might read this and tell Oprah I lied and it's *A Million Little Pieces* all over again, so GET OFF MY BACK ALREADY!

I SUCK — are ya happy now?!

I have already sustained an injury this season that had me miss the past two months of racing. Fellow fundraiser Norma suggested my next book might well be "Tainted Ribs – Diary of a Go-Karter". Perhaps so.

My Buddhist self has allowed me to find divine happenstance with this weakness by concluding that I exist in go-karting mediocrity because being lapped gives confidence to the next Mario Andretti. I exist on the track every other Friday night, rain or shine, to ensure HIS life is blessed.

Time to meditate… uuuuhhhhhmmmmmmmmm.

SIX MONTHS IN A LEAKY BOAT
SPLIT ENZ

Now that I don't have cigarettes to deflect the angst of the minor crises that pop up from time to time, I feel that I should be coddled — you know, handled with kid gloves. You see, I'm in a delicate state now, and my psyche can be very easily crushed under the weight of anything negative.

During this time, I began to realize I knew a lot more about myself as a result of a great deal of self-analysis. I had reached the one-year mark, I was proud of my accomplishment, my book seemed as complete as it would get, and it was time to make a move toward something even more positive.

I did what any other author-wanna-be would do when they've poured out their soul in a diary:

In my quest for positive reinforcing feedback, I took my book, the very essence of my personal feelings for the past year, and touted it among many publishers, whom I envisioned would start a bidding war in order to have the rights to my literary epic.

I waited for the phone to ring off the hook. While I waited, the following happened.

"…this is not to say your work is not valid, merely not within the publishing plans of…"

Say what? …But, are you sure this letter was meant for me? …Oh yes, there it is, on the address line: "Dear author"….

If nothing else, I felt a wee rush to be addressed as an 'author,' even if it was in the context of a form rejection letter.

But rest assured, fledgling writer, there's a long stretch of track between being an author and being a *published* author.

The first half dozen rejections came within the first two weeks. I didn't freak out. In fact, in my head, it went something like this:

"Well, the rejection was so fast in coming, I know it's not that my book proposal turned them off. They barely had time to read it with the response coming back that quickly. So it MUST be that they just aren't accepting *anything* new right now."

In a further attempt at self-redemption, I then went on to think, "It's a shame for them that they didn't take the time to peek at my marketing plan, though. Someday Mr. Publisher-Man will see my book on the bestseller list, and Queen Latifah doing interviews by my side about *Tainted Love – The Movie*, and think to himself — gee, didn't something called *Tainted Love* cross my desk last year?"

And how about the rude ones who didn't even bother to drop the stinkin' form letter in the stinkin' envelope with the six stinkin' bucks worth of pre-paid-by-me postage? What's the matter, too busy shinin' your Nobel Prize for publishing *Dora the Explorer Discovers Another Planet Near Uranus?*

One that almost sent me over the edge was the one that came back with a ripped portion off the back page, mailed back in my six-dollar pre-paid envelope — no note, not a single comment, no form letter, no 'x' or check mark to indicate it had even been looked at. Just the full package minus a three inch piece off the last page.

When I opened that one, I was stunned — I mean jaw-droppin', eyes-poppin' stunned.

I pictured some old fat dude at his big, old fat desk, having just finished a big old fat Philly Cheese steak and he's got a bit of steak stuck between his teeth. So he grabs the nearest thing to him, which would apparently be *Tainted Love: Diary of a Smoker* by Tina Triano, tears a bit off the back, and proceeds to un-wedge the steak from his molars.

I mean, what else is a girl to think? I fear that at that moment, there was a chance that I would succumb to the rejection, and have a mental setback.

As they continued to trickle in, however, over the period of the next six months, (which consequently was the same period that Dr. K. had me weaning off the Prozac entirely), I came to a moment of clarity.

I don't need to get my kudos from the outside world on this one.

Frankly, if I wanted to publish the book so badly, I could print it on my own. I could hire someone to do a website for my book. I could pay someone commission to peddle it to book stores. If nothing else, I can give them away to friends and family because, here's the kicker — the act of *writing the book* is the reward!

> *UM*
> At this point, feel free to hear in the distance the music you heard as you collected your graduation scroll… and the pride you felt on that day… *Tito, hand me a tissue…*

So, needless to say, my ego recovered. I slayed my negativity dragon (I call him Puff…get it? Puff the Magic… like puff of smoke — never mind).

MY book is in YOUR hands at this moment (and, just so I don't get a creepy visual, you do have your clothes on and are holding it with both hands, right…?).

My website has now launched, with feedback I could only have dreamed of a year ago.

In the first 36 hours I had 36 pre-orders… to me that obviously means I have friends who support me because, frankly, they trusted me to deliver on something none of them had seen and many had

TAINTED LOVE

no previous knowledge about.

And somewhere down the road, Queen Latifah may read it, may in fact like it, and let's go for the gold, may in fact direct, produce and star in *Tainted Love – The Movie*.

But if she doesn't, as the song says, *I'm Still Standing* – Elton John.

JUST ANOTHER DAY
OINGO BOINGO

It's been one and a half years since I quit.

I often think back to my quit day and the dark period directly following. If you had told me then that at Q +558 days I would be launching a website and making preparations to publish a book about it all, I would have laughed (and then stabbed you repeatedly with a candy bar because that was pre-Prozac time).

When planning to quit, I knew my environment would remain the same but without cigarettes. My greatest fear was that everything around me would be worse without cigarettes.

I smoked when I read a book, so I better not read a book when I quit....

I smoked when I was angry, so I better not get angry....

TAINTED LOVE

I smoked after sex, so I better not… you get my point.

But alas, here I am at Q+558.

I'm at the same desk, the same computer, in fact, on which I played computer games while chain smoking.

Today I drove my car to work and back — a car that used to be my haven for smoking.

Tonight I'll sip a cocktail with my right hand, and my left hand will be content to tap out the beat of the music playing.

My external environment remained the same, as predicted, but it's not worse without cigarettes — different, but not worse.

I almost never think about cigarettes in that longing way anymore.

Sometimes I think I miss it, for the most fleeting of moments, but mostly now, I really don't.

"Once I ran to you, now I run from you…."

It really was Tainted Love… Goodbye, my lover.

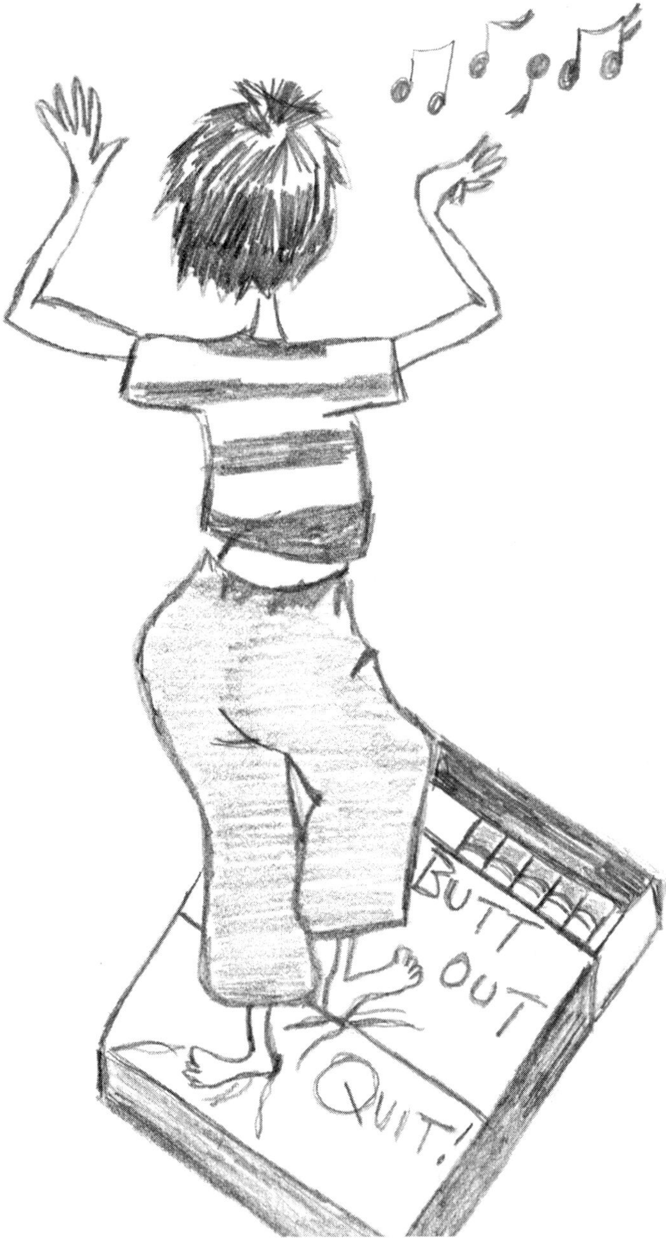
BUTT
OUT
QUIT!

DEDICATION

My mother smoked in a time when smoking was cool.

In 1973, when I was 10 and she was 44, she died of cancer.

As I do my final edit of *Tainted Love* before it goes to print, I take note that this month I turned 44 — the age I have dreaded all my life.

I believe I was not the only one compelled to bring this story to life — and for that I dedicate this book to my mother — Marjorie.

Wish you were here.

August 18, 2006.